Corporate Finance Formulas:

A Simple Introduction

Also by K.H. Erickson

Simple Introductions

Choice Theory
Corporate Finance Formulas
Econometrics
Financial Economics
Game Theory
Game Theory for Business
Investment Appraisal
Microeconomics

Corporate Finance Formulas:

A Simple Introduction

K.H. Erickson

Contents

Risk and Return

Expected return and risk

Expected return, $E(r) = \sum(r_i \times p_i) = \underline{r}$

r_i = a possible return that will occur in a scenario i;

p_i = the probability that a scenario i will occur;

$\sum$ = summation for all levels of i to represent all possible outcomes;

$\underline{r}$ = mean average of all possible returns, weighed by the percentage likelihood of their occurrence.

Variance risk, $\sigma^2(r) = \sum[p_i \times (r_i - \underline{r})^2]$

$\sigma^2(r)$ = the variance of the return, measured by the dispersion of returns around the mean.

Standard deviation risk, $\sigma(r) = \sqrt{\sigma^2(r)}$

$\sigma(r)$ = the standard deviation of the return, measured by the average dispersion of the returns around the expected return.

2 asset portfolio expected return and risk

2 asset portfolio expected return, $E(r_{1,2})$
$= [E(r_1) \times p_1] + [E(r_2) \times p_2]$

$E(r_1)$ = expected return for asset 1;
$E(r_2)$ = expected return for asset 2;
p_1 = the proportion or percentage of the portfolio taken up by asset 1;
p_2 = proportion of the portfolio taken up by asset 2.

2 asset portfolio variance, $\sigma^2(r_{1,2})$
$= [\sigma^2(r_1) \times p_1^2] + [\sigma^2(r_2) \times p_2^2] + [2 \times p_1 \times p_2 \times cov(r_1,r_2)]$
$= [\sigma^2(r_1) \times p_1^2] + [\sigma^2(r_2) \times p_2^2] + [2 \times p_1 \times p_2 \times \rho_{1,2} \times \sigma(r_1) \times \sigma(r_2)]$

$\sigma^2(r_1)$ = variance of the return of asset 1;
$\sigma^2(r_2)$ = variance of the return of asset 2;
$\sigma(r_1)$ = standard deviation of the return of asset 1;
$\sigma(r_2)$ = standard deviation of the return of asset 2;
$cov(r_1,r_2)$ = the covariance between asset 1 returns and asset 2 returns;
$\rho_{1,2}$ = correlation coefficient for asset 1 and asset 2, ranging from -1 (exact negative correlation) to 1 (exact positive correlation).

Returns over time

$$r_{jt} = \alpha_j + (\beta_j \times r_{mt}) + \varepsilon_{jt}$$

r_{jt} = the return of asset j in time period t;
α_j = a constant factor in the return of asset j;
r_{mt} = the market return in time period t;
β_j = beta, a parameter specific to each asset j which shows the sensitivity of the asset j return to changes in the market return. Beta value > 1 magnifies the effect of market return fluctuations, beta < 1 reduces the effect. Beta is the slope in a regression of the return of asset j against the market return;
ε_{jt} = random error in the return of asset j at time period t.

Market and specific risk

$$(\text{Total risk})^2 = (\text{market risk})^2 + (\text{specific risk})^2$$

Total risk for a security j = $\sigma(r_j) = [\beta_j \times \sigma(r_m)] + \sigma(\varepsilon_j)$

Market risk for a security j = $\beta_j \times \sigma(r_m)$
Specific risk for a security j = $\sigma(\varepsilon_j)$

$\sigma(r_m)$ = standard deviation risk of the market return;
$\sigma(\varepsilon_j)$ = standard deviation of the random error of asset j.

Beta coefficient

$$\beta_j = cov(r_j, r_m) / \sigma^2(r_m)$$

β_j = the beta value for asset j, and each different asset will have a different beta value. The portfolio's beta value is a weighted average of all individual asset betas, with the weights the relative value of each stock;
$cov(r_j, r_m)$ = covariance between asset j and market returns;
$\sigma^2(r_m)$ = the variance risk of the market return.

The capital market line: risk-free and risky asset portfolio expected return and risk

A risk-free and risky asset portfolio expected return,
$$E(r_{f,r}) = [r_f \times (1 - p_r)] + [E(r_r) \times p_r]$$
$$= r_f + [(E(r_r) - r_f) \times p_r]$$

r_f = the risk-free return;
$E(r_r)$ = the expected return of the risky asset;

P_r = the percentage the risky asset takes up in the portfolio; $(E(r_r) - r_f)$ = the risk premium, and the excess return the risky asset is expected to give over the risk-free return.

A risk-free asset and risky asset portfolio risk,
$$\sigma(r_{f,r}) = \sigma(r_r) \times p_r$$

$\sigma(r_r)$ = standard deviation risk for the risky asset's return.

A risk-free and risky asset portfolio expected return,
$$E(r_{f,r}) = r_f + \{[\sigma(r_{f,r}) / \sigma(r_r)] \times (E(r_r) - r_f)\}$$

If the risky asset is the market portfolio then the last formula becomes the formula for the capital market line:

The capital market line, expected return for a portfolio containing a risk-free asset and the market portfolio,
$$E(r_p) = r_f + [\sigma_p / \sigma_m] \times (E(r_m) - r_f)$$

$E(r_p)$ = the portfolio's expected return;
$E(r_m)$ = the return of the market portfolio;
σ_p = the portfolio's standard deviation risk;
σ_m = standard deviation of the market portfolio's returns;
/ = divided by.

Cost of Equity

The capital asset pricing model (CAPM)

Capital asset pricing model,
$$E(r_j) = r_f + [\beta_j \times (E(r_m) - r_f)]$$

$E(r_j)$ = expected return of asset j, and CAPM expected return also equals the required rate of return, $E(r) = k$;

r_f = risk-free rate of return;

β_j = the beta of asset j, which represents the stock's sensitivity to changes in the returns of the market portfolio. The beta value represents systematic non-diversifiable risk, and while some risk may be eliminated with a diversified portfolio, non-diversifiable risk can't be reduced and a higher beta raises the required (expected) rate of return;

$(E(r_m) - r_f)$ = the market risk premium, equity risk premium.

Equity risk premium, $(E(r_m) - r_f) = \sigma^2_m \times A$

σ^2_m = variance of the market portfolio's returns;

A = weighted average of risk aversion of wealth-holders.

Holding period return

Holding period return, $HPR_t = (P_t - P_{t-1} + Div_t) / P_{t-1}$

HPR_t, the average holding period return is the average cost of equity, k_E;
P_t = the price of the asset at time t, the end of the holding period;
P_{t-1} = the price of the asset at time t-1, the start of the holding period;
Div_t = the dividend for the time period.

Adjusting returns for inflation

$r_{real} = [(1 + r_{nominal}) / (1 + inflation)] - 1$

r_{real} = average real rate of return after adjusting for inflation;
$r_{nominal}$ = the nominal rate of return before inflation.

$k_E = [(1 + average\ r_{real}) \times (1 + expected\ inflation)] - 1$

k_E = the cost of equity.

Accounting cost of equity

k_E(unlevered) = ROI x (1 - T_C)

k_E = k_E(unlevered) + {[k_E(unlevered) - k_D] x (1 - T_C) x (D/E)}

k_E(unlevered) = the cost of equity after debts are paid;
ROI = the accounting return on investment;
(1 - T_C) = after tax, where T_C is the corporate tax rate;
k_D = the cost of debt;
D/E = targeted debt-to-equity ratio.

Dividend discount model

Assuming constant dividend growth and cost of equity, and that the latter exceeds the former, and a constant D/E:

P_0 = [Div_0 x (1 + g)] / (k_E - g)

k_E = ([Div_0 x (1 + g)] / P_0) + g

g = ROE x (1 - Payout)

Div_0 = dividend for the current period;

g = dividend growth rate;

P_0 = price for the current period;

Payout = the dividend ratio paid out in dividends to shareholders;

ROE = return on equity, net income / shareholder's equity.

Price-earnings (P/E) model

$$k_E = ([Payout \times EPS_0 \times (1 + g)] / P_0) + g$$
$$= ([Payout \times (1 + g)] / [P_0 / EPS_0]) + g$$

EPS_0 = earnings per share for the current period.

The price-earnings model follows the same assumptions as the dividend discount model.

Cost of Capital

CAPM cost of capital

Cost of capital, $k = r_f + [\beta_A \times (r_m - r_f)]$

B_A = beta of assets, beta for company's assets combined.

Beta of assets of a company

$B_A = \{B_E \times [V_E / (V_E + V_D)]\} + \{B_D \times [V_D / (V_E + V_D)]\}$
$B_A = \{B_E + [B_D \times (V_D / V_E)]\} / [1 + (V_D / V_E)]$

B_E = the beta of equity, the beta value for all equity assets;
B_D = the beta value of debt, the beta value for all debt assets;
V_E = the market value of equity assets;
V_D = the market value of net debt assets.

A company with little debt has a debt beta approximately equal to zero, and the above formula becomes:

$$B_A = B_E / [1 + (V_D / V_E)]$$

With taxes (T_C) the beta of assets for a company is:

$$B_A = \{B_E + [B_D \times (1 - T_C) \times (V_D / V_E)]\} / \{1 + [(1 - T_C) \times (V_D / V_E)]\}$$

And with both taxes and a company with little debt for a debt beta value of approximately zero:

$$B_A = B_E / \{1 + [(1 - T_C) \times (V_D / V_E)]\}$$

Weighted average cost of capital (WACC)

Without taxes:

Cost of capital, k or WACC = $\{k_E \times [V_E / (V_E + V_D)]\}$ + $\{k_D \times [V_D / (V_E + V_D)]\}$

With taxes:

Cost of capital, k or WACC = $\{k_E \times [V_E / (V_E + V_D)]\}$ + $\{k_D \times (1 - T_C) \times [V_D / (V_E + V_D)]\}$

Market value of debt

Estimated market value of debt, V_D
= annual interest expenses $\times$ {(1 - [1 / (1 + current YTM)$^{\text{maturity of debt}}$]) / current YTM}

YTM = yield to maturity.

Cost of capital in emerging markets

In emerging markets risk-free assets may not exist, but their cost of capital can be found using another country's data. E.g. emerging market of Chile may use data from the US:

Chilean cost of capital, k
= $r_{f,US} + (r_{gb,CH} - r_{f,US}) + (\beta_e \times rp_{US})$

$r_{f,US}$ = US risk-free rate;
rp_{US} = US risk premium;
$r_{gb,CH}$ = government bond rate in Chile;
$(r_{gb,CH} - r_{f,US})$ = sovereign spread, difference in bond yields between Chile and risk-free US, a proxy for political risk;
β_e = beta for the relevant sector of activity in the US.

However, this will calculate the Chilean cost of capital in US dollars, and another formula is needed to switch this to Chilean pesos:

Cost of capital in Chilean pesos, k
= {(1 + cost of capital in $US) / [(1 + inflation rate in US) / (1 + inflation rate in Chile)]} - 1

Private company beta value

A private company won't have a market value like a public firm on the stock market, and in this scenario an investor will be concerned with total risk and not just market risk. Beta is adjusted to represent total risk as follows:

Total beta = (Total risk / Market risk) x β = (1 / R^2) x β

Market risk = systematic or diversifiable risk;
R^2 = the goodness of fit value from a regression, representing how accurately a regression formula explains the sample data. R^2 ranges from 0 (completely inaccurate) to 1 (perfectly accurate).

Capital Structure

Modigliani and Miller (MM) theorem

The first MM proposition states that in perfect capital markets, and without taxation, a company's value is the same whether levered (with debt) or unlevered (no debt):

$$V_L = V_U$$

V_L = the value of a levered company;
V_U = the value of an unlevered company.

The second proposition states that changing the leverage on total cash flows doesn't change the weighted average cost of capital, and the cost of equity (k_E) will balance it out:

$$k_E = k_{EU} + [(k_{EU} - k_D) \times (V_D / V_E)]$$

k_{EU} = cost of equity for unlevered (without debt) company;
k_D = cost of debt;
V_D = value of debt;
V_E = value of equity.

The benefits of debt

Interest expenses on debt may be tax free and this will offer a benefit to using debt over equity in capital structure. If tax savings are permanent the cost of debt is used to discount tax savings:

Value of tax savings $= (T_C \times k_D \times V_D) / k_D = T_C \times V_D$

T_C = the corporate tax rate.

And as the debt levels and tax savings on interest may change, as may tax rates, tax savings might also be discounted using the cost of equity or the WACC.

MM theorem with corporate taxes

Including corporate taxes changes the first MM proposition, and the cost of equity:

$$V_L = V_U + (T_C \times V_D)$$

$$k_E = k_{EU} + [(k_{EU} - k_D) \times (1 - T_C) \times (V_D / V_E)]$$

Personal taxes

Personal taxes for investors on interest income and dividends can cancel out the benefits of debt with corporate taxes. Personal taxes change the overall tax shield:

Tax shield, $G = [1 - \{[(1 - T_C) \times (1 - T_E)] / (1 - T_D)\}] \times V_D$

T_C = corporate tax rate;
T_D = personal tax rate on interest income;
T_E = personal tax rate on dividends;
If $T_E = T_D$ the tax shield is as with only corporate taxes;
If $T_E > T_D$ the tax shield is bigger than original scenario;
If $T_E < T_D$ the tax shield is smaller than original scenario.

The costs of debt

A highly levered firm with large amounts of debt will face costs of financial distress that reduce its value:

$V_L = V_U + PV$ of tax shield - PV of financial distress and bankruptcy costs

PV = present value, as future cash flows are discounted.

Expected costs of financial distress = pD x CFD

pD = probability of financial distress or bankruptcy;
CFD = costs of financial distress or bankruptcy.

Adding the tax shield and costs of financial distress to the value of a levered firm gives the adjusted present value of the costs of debt:

$$V_L = V_U + G - (pD \times CFD)$$

Payout Policy

Organic growth

BV of equity y_0 + retained earnings = BV of equity y_1

BV = book value;
y_0 = beginning of the year;
y_1 = end of the year;
Retained earnings are those not paid out on dividends.

Internal growth

With constant capital structure and price / book value:

ROE = ROCE + [(ROCE - i) x D/E]

ROE = return on book value of equity;
ROCE = return on capital employed;
i = after tax cost of debt;
D/E = debt-to-equity ratio.

With the payout ratio this gives the internal growth model:

$$g = \{ROCE + [(ROCE - i) \times D/E]\} \times (1 - d)$$

g = growth rate of capital employed;
d = dividend payout ratio, dividend / net profit.

With a leveraged buyout, where debt is used by a firm to finance an acquisition of another firm, the growth rate of capital is also influenced by the tax rate and tax consolidation is a leading driver of the process:

$$g = \{ROCE + [(ROCE - i(1 - T_C)) \times D/E]\} \times (1 - d)$$

Financing

External financing = Retained earnings - [change in sales $\times$ (capital employed / sales)]

Assuming there isn't a capital increase the following holds:

(Change in net profit / net profit) =
[(change in net profit / change in book value of equity)
$\times$ **(change in book equity / net profit)]**

Growth rate of earnings = marginal rate of return on equity x **(1 - d)**

Change in net profit = growth of FCF x **(V_D / V_E)**

FCF = free cash flows, operating cash flow - capital expenditure.

Dilution of control

The dilution of control is the reduction in control in the company which a shareholder faces, where a capital increase sees neither an inflow nor an outflow of funds. It occurs when old shareholders don't subscribe to the issue of new shares in proportion to their current level of shareholding.

In the absence of subscription rights the dilution of control for a shareholder is given by the formula:

Dilution of control = N_1 / (N_0 + N_1)

N_0 = no. of old shares;
N_1 = no. of new shares.

With a rights issue this formula only gives the apparent dilution, and subscription rights allow shareholders to partially participate in the capital increase with no fund outlay. The actual dilution of control will be less than the apparent dilution.

The real dilution is the dilution of control attributed solely to the capital increase, independent of subscription rights:

Real dilution of control = proceeds of capital increase / (value of equity before capital increase + proceeds of capital increase)

And another method can also calculate the real dilution:

Real dilution of control = $n_1 / (N_0 + n_1)$

n_1 = represents the number of shares that would be issued if the issue price was equal to the market value of the shares:

n_1 = proceeds of capital increase / market value of each share

And the difference between the apparent dilution of control and the real dilution is called the technical dilution:

Technical dilution= apparent dilution - real dilution

Technical dilution is the additional dilution caused by shareholders selling subscription rights after the capital increase, taking the opportunity to reduce their investment in the company.

Capital increase and earnings per share

Change in EPS = {(P/E) x (capital raised / market cap. after capital increase) x [after tax rate of return - (E/P)]}

EPS = earnings per share;
P/E = price-earnings ratio;
Market cap. = market capitalization, the total value of all shares, share price x no. of shares;
E/P = earnings-price ratio.

P/E ratio = market capitalization / net income
E/P ratio = net income / market capitalization

Valuation

Future and present value

Future value = V $(1 + i)^n$

Present value = Future value / $(1 + i)^n$

V = the value of the sum of money invested;
i = the rate of interest for a period;
n = the number of periods the money is invested.

Change in value

Percentage change in value = [(V x ERR) / RRR] - V

V = the value of the sum of money invested;
ERR = the expected rate of return;
RRR = the required rate of return, also known as the cost of capital, k.

Firm value and free cash flows

$$V = V_E + V_D = \sum [FCF_t / (1 + k)^t]$$

V = enterprise value or firm value;

V_E = value of equity;

V_D = value of debt;

$\sum$ = summation across all values from 1 to t;

t = time period;

FCF = expected free cash flows;

k = cost of capital.

Free cash flow calculation

FCF = EBIT - T + DA - Ce - change in WC

EBIT = Operating income, earnings before interest and taxation;

T = normalized tax on operating income;

DA = depreciation and amortization;

Ce = capital expenditure;

WC = working capital.

Gordon-Shapiro formula for total firm value

TV = normalized FCF / (k - g)

TV = total firm value;
k = cost of capital or required rate of return;
g = growth rate of normalized cash flow to perpetuity.

Earnings multiples

First capital employed is calculated:

Capital employed = market capitalization + value of debt

Where market capitalization is the value of equity.

With capital employed earnings multiples can be found:

EBIT multiple = capital employed / EBIT

EBITDA multiple = capital employed / EBITDA

EBITDA = earnings before interest, taxes, depreciation and amortization.

NOPAT multiple = capital employed / NOPAT

NOPAT = EBIT (1 - T_C)

NOPAT = net operating profit after taxes;
T_C = tax rate.

Mergers

Relative ownership

In a merger between two firms the acquiring firm may be denoted as firm A, and the target or acquired firm as firm B. After the merger the relative ownership of firm A in the new firm is:

$$V_A / (V_A + V_B) = 1 / [1 + (V_B / V_A)]$$

And the relative ownership of firm B in the new firm after the merger is given by:

$$V_B / (V_A + V_B) = (V_B / V_A) / [1 + (V_B / V_A)]$$

V_A = value of firm A;
V_B = value of firm B.

The relative ownership levels give a relative value ratio, and with this an exchange ratio can be found. This is the ratio of the number of shares of company A that are to be delivered for each share received from company B.

Exchange ratio (A/B) = relative value ratio x (premerger no. of A shares / premerger no. of B shares)

Premerger no. of A shares = the total number of shares firm A had in the market before the merger;
Premerger no. of B shares = the total number of shares firm B had in the market before the merger.